MR VOLE'S UPSIDE-DOWN NEW POTS

In memory of
The Heathcote School Stevenage – Where a brilliant teacher
gave me a fantastic remembering technique
– the inspiration for this book!

rhymingmoments.co.uk
First published 2022 by Rhyming Moment's books
61 Bridge Street, Kington HR5 3DJ

ISBN: 978-1-9196188-6-9

Text copyright © Trudy Davidson 2022
Illustrations copyright © Melanie Mitchell 2022
The rights of Trudy Davidson and Melanie Mitchell to be
identified as the author and illustrator of this work
have been asserted in accordance with the
Copyright, Designs and Patents Act 1988.

All rights reserved. No part of this publication may be
reproduced, stored in a retrieval system or transmitted
in any form, or by any means (electronic, mechanical,
photocopying, recording or otherwise), without the prior
written permission of the publisher.

A CIP catalogue for this book is
available from the British Library
upon request.

MR VOLE'S

UPSIDE-DOWN

NEW

POTS

Written by
Trudy Davidson

Illustrated by
Melanie Mitchell

Ollie was a tawny owl, the wisest bird in Broadleaf Wood. He could answer any question and his answers were known to be good.

Animals large and small would come to see Ollie for advice. He loved the attention, and the gifts he received in return were also rather nice.

Pots for Sale

In the tangled roots of Ollie's tree, a little brown vole watched the visitors as he squeaked with glee! Although risky, he set up home in this perfect spot, as he saw an opportunity to sell his new leafy pots.

Much to Ollie's delight and surprise, he had seen the vole's peeping eyes. Having a tasty snack right at his door, he quickly flew down to the shady floor.

He was met by a shop of upside-down pots, cleverly made by twisting leaves into knots.

"Hello!" hooted Ollie, peering through a pot with a gap, where the vole sat with his paws in his lap.

"Hello!" replied the vole, as calm as can be. "I have an idea that could help you and me!"

Ollie jumped backwards in surprise. "Let me hear it!" Ollie said, with curious eyes.
The vole smiled and said, "I will lay tracks so your tree can be found, and in return I will sell my new pots that you see on the ground."

Ollie knew his tree was hard to find, so thought this offer was rather kind. He replied, "OK Mr Vole, you have a deal. I will not make you my tasty meal!"
Mr Vole and Ollie shook wing and paw, then as Ollie turned to leave the shady floor, Mr Vole squeaked loudly, "Do you really know the answer to everything?"

Ollie looked back over his wing and said, "Well...I can get muddled by what is in our sky." And off he flew, with a wave goodbye.
A sly fox was near that night, and when he heard them talking, his eyes shone bright.

A queue of animals started forming, full of questions for the morning. Ollie gave a loud, "Twit-twoo," and up to his branch he swiftly flew.

A little deer came forward first and bleated, "When will I grow antlers like my dad? Not having any makes me so sad."
Ollie leant forward. "By the time you are one, your antlers will grow. Be patient, they will be wonderful when they show."

The deer thanked Ollie and left feeling pleased, handing over some berry juice his mum had freshly squeezed.

A grey squirrel was next and squeaked, "Tell me, please, what can I do? When I collect nuts, I can only hold a few."
Ollie smiled and swiftly said, "A vole sells pots at the bottom of this tree, buy the biggest one you can see!" Ollie stretched one wing out towards the tree base, where Mr Vole stood with a big grin on his face.
The squirrel gave a big smile and thanked Ollie with a large bag of nuts that would last a while.

A young hedgehog shuffled to the front, gave a tiny grunt and said, "How many spines do I have please? I have tried to count, but it is taking a long time to sum up all these!"

Ollie grinned and said, "It is great seeing all your spines when you turn into a ball, but the number is not the same for all. You could have up to seven thousand covering your back and sides. This would take you a long time to sum up if you tried!"

The hedgehog was happy she no longer needed to count her spines for hours and left Ollie some lovely flowers.

The sly fox was next. He was jealous of the attention Ollie received, and had arrived with a plan to stop it, he believed. The fox stroked his tail and fluffed it with his nail as he slowly leant foward and said, "What is the order of the planets in our sky? I would really love to hear your reply!"

Ollie took a big breath in and rubbed the tip of his wing on his chin.

The fox must have heard him answer Mr Vole's question about the sky - oh why, oh why, did he not just lie!

Mr Vole was friends with a clever dragonfly, who had told him about the wonders in the sky.

Hiding on the twig above Ollie's ear, he whispered, "You do know this one, have a think. What I sell on the ground is the link!"

Ollie was confused and turned his head whilst he slowly thought about what the vole had said. "What help are Mr Vole's pots?" he mumbled. "There is Mercury, Earth, Venus...no...the order is still jumbled."

Then, all of a sudden, the owl laughed as he realised he knew; the vole had given him the most wonderful clue!

He continued to laugh, and then laughed some more. He laughed so much his tummy was sore.

"The answer is right in front of me, covered in knots.
Mr Vole earns money just selling upside-down new pots!
Is the order of the planets above us at night! Yes, yes, that is definitely right!"

The sly fox gave the biggest grin. "That's nothing to do with planets in the sky!" The animals all gasped.
"Ollie doesn't know. Oh my, oh my! Ollie is no longer the wisest guy!"

"Wait!" said Ollie. "Take the first letter of each word in the sentence in your head –M, V, E, M, J, S, U, N– and this is the order of the planets that you seek. It also gives you a fantastic remembering technique!"

The fox's grin changed to a look of disbelief, whilst Ollie and the vole were both smiling with relief. The fox dropped his tail, his face turned pale and through gritted teeth he slowly said, "Fantastic Ollie, I am so pleased you knew the answer!" as the line of animals watched with relief and laughter.

The fox quickly disappeared knowing he was not leaving for good. He would try another way to be the wisest animal in Broadleaf Wood.

Mr Vole continues to live in the roots of Ollie's tree, but his pots are now the right way round, you see. They have agreed that they make a good team, and they often enjoy spending time by the stream.

They always laugh about the day the fox was up to no good, and how helping each other still made Ollie the wisest in Broadleaf Wood.

www.ingramcontent.com/pod-product-compliance
Lightning Source LLC
Chambersburg PA
CBHW051250110526
44588CB00025B/2942